Interactive Press

Afterglow

Born in the UK, raised in the US, Laura Jan Shore immigrated to Australia in 1996 and has lived on the Far North Coast of New South Wales ever since. Her previous poetry collections include *Breathworks* (Dangerously Poetic Press, 2002) and *Water over Stone*, IP Picks Best Poetry 2011, Interactive Press. Her YA novel, *The Sacred Moon Tree* (Bradbury Press, 1986) was nominated for the Washington Irving Children's Book Award. Her work has been published in anthologies and literary journals on four continents including *Aesthetica*, *Magma* and *The Best Australian Poems* (2013).

Her readings have included *Poetica* on Radio National, The Brett Whitely reading series, the Hudson Valley Writer's Center in NY, Perth Poetry Club, the Sydney Writers Festival, Byron Bay Writers Festival and Queensland Poetry Festival. She's held residencies at New Pacific Studio, New Zealand, KSP Writers Centre in Perth, Varuna in the Blue Mts. and the Poets on Wheels tour, 2003.

President of Dangerously Poetic Press, she co-edited 13 books and has facilitated poetry readings since 2000. She has been teaching creative writing and poetry since 1980.

After her husband's sudden death, she felt compelled to piece together the mosaic of contradictions—his enigmatic character and the love that saw them through: marriage, divorce, five years on separate continents and then re-marriage for an additional thirteen years. To write about this, she needed support. She enrolled in the MFA program at Pacific University, Portland, Oregon where she had the privilege to work with some of her favourite poets such as: Dorianne Laux, Joseph Millar, Sandra Alcosser, Kwame Dawes and Ellen Bass. In June, 2019 she received her MFA in Creative Writing and completed the manuscript for *Afterglow*.

Poetry brings solace and renewal in a chaotic world. Laura will continue to encourage local community building through poetry. Her dream is to find fresh ways to connect poets and poetry lovers so they might nourish and sustain each other in a global community.

Interactive Press
Brisbane

Afterglow

Laura Jan Shore

Interactive Press

Interactive Press
an imprint of IP (Interactive Publications Pty Ltd)
Treetop Studio • 9 Kuhler Court
Carindale, Queensland, Australia 4152
sales@ipoz.biz
http://ipoz.biz/

Printed in 14 pt Chalet Medium on 14 pt Avenir Book.

ISBN: 9781922332219 (PB); 9781922332226 (eBk)

a catalogue record of this book is available
from the National Library of Australia

for Anand

Acknowledgements

Front cover image: Laura Jan Shore

Jacket Design: David Reiter, Jodie Clowes

Author photo: Annelies Kaufman

Grateful acknowledgement is made to all the teachers and students at the Pacific University MFA program especially: Dorianne Laux, Emily Ransdell and Megan Welsh on my thesis committee. Your feedback and encouragement was invaluable. Thanks to all the poets, living and dead, whose work sustained me through my darkest hours. Special thanks to my friends, Annelies Kaufman and Nathalie Verdejo for their support with the cover and photo. Also, to Jodie Clowes for her perceptive design. Thanks to Varuna for residencies in 2016 and 2018, providing precious space and time for developing this work.

Thanks to the editors of the following publications where some of these poems originally appeared:

"Upon Waking", under previous title, "Grief", *Grieve*, Hunter Valley Writers Centre, New South Wales, 2016.

"First Anniversary", *Grieve*, Vol. 5, Hunter Valley Writers Centre, 2017. Winner of The Calvary Mater Hospital Pastoral Care Award,

"Vanished", *Grieve*, Vol. 7, Hunter Valley Writers Centre, 2019.

"Small Gusts of Suffering", *Empathy*, Poems from the Australian Catholic University Prize for Poetry, Melbourne, 2018.

"Don't Say it", *The Same*, Vol.10, No.1, Mt. Union, PA. 2012.

"Again", *Poetry Chaikhana* – online http://www.poetry-chaikhana.com

"In Praise of Foibles", "Our Covenant", "Prelude to an Afternoon Nap", *The Blue Nib Literary Magazine*, January 2020.

Contents

1

Even the meantime, which is the holy time

of being on earth in overlapping lifetimes, ends.

– Galway Kinnell, from *When One Has Lived a Long Time Alone*

Visitations

Ours is a fractured romance. We appear
to each other in so many disguises.
You stumble on the beach and presto,
we're two French soldiers in a trench
touching fingers in a rain of mud and blood.
We might be making love when, in the pale light
of dusk, your ecstasy becomes
a killer's mask. I wrestle back my scream.
When the weight of your need collapses me,
you are the infant, chewing on the sinews of my heart.
Like shadows, they're an overlay
upon the day we're living, a transfiguration.

No one knows how many times we're born
or why, life after life, this joy and devastation.

Nocturne in Blue

Mutable as a cloud
sculpted by wind, I didn't
understand the boundaries of skin.

Then the heat of your hands,
a cradle for my cheeks,
fingertips at my brow,

how you tilted
my face, left to right,
like holding rare fruit.

Our lips almost touching as we hummed,
we played with oscillation and pitch,
until our notes met and split and met again.

A kind of mating in mid-air,
voice to voice,
intimate as sex.

I mortgaged half my life for this,
willing to ride the chaos of your moods
just to steep in those rare pools of resonance.

After you died, I listened deep
into the night until I heard
the frequency of us.

Now your absence reverberates
through my cells, the shush-shush
of the sea seeping through the blinds.

Upon Waking

A full-bodied NO
flutes

through the hollows
of my bones, oboes

my blood.
This one-sided argument
colonizes my days.

Even my fingernails crack
at the shock of it.

Our symphony flattens and thins.
Nights swirl empty
of stars.

Dust slams my windows,
scrapes under my doors.

My mouth is a desert.
Grit coats my teeth.

My ears throb
with listening.

Your silence,
my uproar.

How Did He Die?

He died—because of the flu,
I mean, the flu caused fluids
to mass around his heart.
He thought it was pneumonia.
He couldn't take a deep breath.

His heart was OK—so they
discharged him from hospital.

He died—from a panic attack.
No, it was panic
that sent him back
to the ER
where an intern learned
the hospital had taken him off
his meds for bi-polar,
the ones that seemed to work,
but this was Texas
and they didn't use that brand—so
he was put on a new pill
but because the number one
side effect was suicide,
the doctor made him sign a pact
with his brother not to do it.

He died—because he was tired
and he couldn't sleep,
no, because he thought
he was dying anyway,
slowly, the pain
around his heart, he couldn't
take a deep breath.

He died—because he
didn't want to wait.

Ascending Mt. Jerusalem

Why this urgent fever
to scramble up and over, blood
ringing my ears, tremor
in my legs?

I stare at the cliffs, rise
through red cedars
and lemon scented gums. Gather
dusky coral peas and a parrot feather
to place at the top.

To taste your lips
I lick my own.

Do you hear the crunch
of pebbles? Remember how
knees and ankles crackle, the pinch
of toes inside boots?

On the wind, a whiff
of your musk.

Through the mayhem
of cicadas, a scarf of mist,

I hoist my body
into cloud.

Is this heaven then, smudged
edges and muffled noise?
I sprawl against granite.

All this climbing for the vista
and I'm enveloped
in swells of fog, dizzy
with loss.

Vanishing

On the lawn this morning, a lump
of faded feathers. A parrot
nudges his limp mate.

All day, he waits
for those green wings
to flex and follow.

A bruise blooms
on my breastbone.
Everywhere couples:

heads angled
towards each other,
hands finding other hands.

I touch your talc grey ashes
to my tongue. Grit fails
to still the tumbling in my chest.

Curled on my side of the bed,
I picture your iris—
opalescent, beckoning.

I was baptised in your gaze,
the beam
of your affection.

When your lids closed,
the woman you saw
vanished.

No Refuge

I wish I'd been there
when you were a cross-eyed child
forever losing your glasses in Depew Park,
your father marching you back to the apple sapling,
thick lenses dangling from a branch.

You balked at desks and books.
Your paradise was damming up streams
and riding small pines in the wind.

All the falls and breaks.
The woods where the hemlock split
thrusting you to the rocks and the driveway,
where you knelt examining
a nest of ants, the scar
on your ankle
where the truck drove over it.

What lay beneath? Trounced
by bullies, your quirky gifts and shifts
of mood misunderstood.
Blame can breed fury
But, in you, it was bewilderment.

Where is the kindness here?
You switched off the TV news
with its shock and awe wars,
and planted Christmas trees for solace.

Your *Jain* phase when you refused
to wear shoes
or anything made of leather. You
flinched as each footfall crushed soil microbes.

A bee vibrating a pink bloom reminded you
how many flowers
never fruited anymore. How even
the spring sun scalds.

Born to defile the garden, this creed of dominion
bred into us. How to recast
this ancient tale?

When a tree falls in the forest, it's swarmed.
Lichens, fungi, rodents and insects
devour it, bark to pith, nothing's left
but mulch.

The word, *paradise,* is old
Persian, meaning *walled garden.*
Rumpled and weary, you groped for the gate.

On the gnarled tree, a lone apple,
cankered and brown, clings
past its season. I feel your hand
on my shoulder and stare up,
searching the clouds.

First Anniversary

Outside my window, the you-you-you
of mourning doves and I wake, bewildered.
The redwoods hold each other up
below the soil, intertwined.

On your side of the bed I've spread
a felled tree's worth of poetry.
The mulch of memory.

Your stopped breath still
saturates my lungs.
In the night, the moans that startle me
are my own.

Each room where you are not,
your things imprinted with your touch,
I gather into piles to give away or toss.

I carry that spark
my heartwood.
Where do our high-voltage fingers
find each other in the dark?

No Good-bye for Ducks

One year has passed
and no one
has ever called me *widow*.
Not a black armband in sight.
No bells tolled.
No mirrors or clocks
were draped.

I walk
to his favourite duck pond
and all the birds
begin to cackle.
I gave myself one year, now
I'm bargaining for two.
I've squandered the urge
to rip my clothes and chop
off all my hair.

Now, it's business as usual.

Crouched on the beach, I sculpt
a sand husband
and with my fists, pound him
                into the shore.

II

Lovers don't finally meet somewhere.
They're in each other all along.

– Mawlana Jalal-al-Din Rumi (translated by Coleman Barks)

Refractions

Skin
    does not contain her.

At birth, she fills
    the whole hospital.

Nothing is static.

Expressions, fluid
    as time, flick past.

The eye roams.
    A continuum.

In her mirror, strangers
    startle and dissolve.

Her face,
    a temporary refuge.

Her eyes are the prisms
    his light flares through.

The damp forest of her breath
    is history heaved through her lungs.

She touches her own cheek in wonder.

Collision at the Ashram

Frankincense and chai
enticed me.
The stairs were steep and dimly lit.

Half-listening
to the banter of strangers,
I descended, my eyes
on my feet until I slammed

into his solid flesh,
and was caught
in his glint of recognition.

He clasped my hand as if
he'd always held it
and steered me
through the crowd to a quiet corner.

You look terrific! The surprise
of my own words
saturated the space between us.

Only then did I step back
to soak in
the weight he'd lost and his tender grin,
his new turtleneck, still creased from the packet.

I'd never seen him
without paint-spattered overalls,
or his beard
without a sprinkle of sawdust.

Sandalwood mala beads dangled from his neck.
He'd replaced the Guru's photo
with a mirror, a flash
of my own flushed face in it.

First Night

She was on her knees straddling him,
her loose hair cresting over his chest.
It felt like he'd always crooned
slightly off key in her ear,
as he nuzzled the nape
of her neck, examined the creases
in her palm, rapt
as if she were the pony
he'd begged for each Christmas as a boy.
He ran his calloused thumb
across her lips and she suckled it,
his knuckle salty, then a little sweet.

His plush thighs pillowed hers.
She draped the sheets
over their heads, his musk
like forest loam, his hands at home
steering her hips.
Together, the shattering.
She was unabashed by the animal
sounds she'd made
and when he said, *I love you*,
his voice rumbling
as if up from an underground cave,
(that phrase her mother dared not utter,

all she'd needed to hear as a child)
she felt it resound and swell, saturating
her every thirsting cell.

No Doubt

His belly was a dance floor
in a former life, feet pounding jigs
on worn, pine boards
stretched across his navel,
his eyes two bronze-tinted mirrors.
This Swami is a carpenter,
meditates on his lunch hour,
sprawls on the hood of an old blue Ford.
All day he hums
his *I know nothing* waltz,
summoning soft rains
for the parched plains of Africa,
for us, balmy winter nights.
You want Spring? I'll give you, Spring.
Conjuror of cartoon crows, yellow
beaked and sassy, he bellows
their Walt Disney jive
from rafters as he hammers,
each Zen blow in perfect pitch.
Quitting time, he snaps maroon suspenders
dressed in blue jeans and saw dust.

The Faces

It just slipped out at dinner
about the faces.

The Indian's my favourite, I said,
watching the arc
of my father's cheekbones and nose
stretch into the profile on the nickel.

I spoke nothing of the sullen-jowled girl
who appeared as I passed him the salt.
Silence crackled. My stomach flailed
under the scalpel of their stare,
the strange bark of my father's laugh.

Brushing my teeth, I'd search the mirror
with a soft gaze until my own reflection
dissolved into the boy
in a sailor suit. I named him Seymour.
There you are, spray of red hair and pale lashes,
but already melting into the glower
of a wrinkled- lipped woman.

As each face wafted by
I was curious, but shy,
afraid to break the spell,
to dare to ask them, who are you
who gape at me through my own eyes?

Don't be vain. My mother nudged me away
to glance at her lipstick.

Unmentioned over thirty years,
it slipped out again about the faces,
this time to my new lover,
lying beneath me indulging my gaze. His features

a cartoon flicker of images.
Jutting jaw of a moustachioed soldier, fleshy trumpeter's lips,
the eggplant skin of a warrior.
He touched my cheek as I described these men,
no glimmer of disbelief.

Still sprawled on the rug before the fire,
a coy liquorice-eyed girl became a pallid crone
and he said, *Now you're seeing women's faces, aren't you?*

How did you know? I wondered
and he said, *I'm letting them out.*

On the Clock

His tongue
slides left across his lips, slides right
as he measures the floorboard,
rips it with his buzz saw,
then fits row by row
tongue-in-groove together,
nailing each secret into place.

Next the architraves
for the windows, his beard flung
to one side as he steadies the frame
with his chin.

He is haunted by the winter
after his first wife left him,
when the water pipes froze,
how he was on a roof, crying,
trying to tie down a tarp
before snowfall, before dark,
knowing how broke he'd be
if he blew that job,
two kids waiting at home
for him to fix
some sort of supper.

Proposal

Because Ethiopian children were starving,
he put the ladder up against the house
and invited me to climb.

From the rooftop was a view
of the Hudson River I'd never seen.
Because the emaciated bodies, bulbous heads,
we saw on TV haunted him,
he proposed:

a benefit wedding,
a pot-luck open house wedding,
donations to *Save the Children*.

Stunned, I said the only thing I could say.
Let's meditate.
We settled into silence.

When I finally looked out to a sky streaked
apricot and hibiscus, his eyes,
the copper tones of the river, spilled
down the runnels of his cheeks.

May our nuptials
nourish strangers and friends,

a promise.

Paperweights

Chunk of glass spun smooth,
confetti of colour
capturing light,

weighed down
the bills on his desk.
He lived to order
and staple, a display of industry,
the loans, bill of sale,
taxes.

He collected them wherever
we travelled. The first—

his mother gave him, surface
scratched and pitted,
his fascination as a kid,
adept at spinning it across
the coffee table, tossed
and wrestled from his siblings' grasp.

When the reckoning
did not line up, papers rustling
in the breeze, he'd stare for hours
into the frozen swirls,
that beckoning galaxy,

glass globe cradled
in his large
and battered hands.

Sunday Morning Ritual

after Anna Swir

Lovemaking to the fiddle,
banjo and guitar—
we don't need a caller.

The contra-dance swirl,
box the gnat, half-sashay.
Click of heels on sprung floors.
My moony eyes, your crooked grin,
spinning me out, tugging me in.

We dip and swing that final waltz,
me, always a beat ahead,
kick off the sheets, breathe in ¾ time.
Ribald as fresh snow.
Wise as a honky-tonk piano.

All the moos and squawks of the barnyard.
Turn up the music—
or we'll scare the neighbours.

The Perfect Husband

I can never hide
the other man from you,
he, who I glimpse, while you sleep.
Shadowing you, his
head cocked, a little sweaty
at the brow, he lends your eyes
their glint and feeds you jokes.
He's the one who likes to finish chores
and tidy up, the one who brings me
roses, tongues my toes.
Certain mornings, a whiff
of salt-spray
and you wake glued
to him, a perfect meld.
I press the length of my body
into your back, to hold you
both in place.

Wife of the Pied Piper

I was always envious.
No matter where
we travelled, he, a lodestone,
captivated children,
the hidden sprite inside
this hulk of a man.

He would touch their small heads,
fingertips dancing through
their hair, *watch out, it's snowing,*
getting slippery
on the top of the mountain.
Avalanche!

Fingers
tumbling, skittering
down their squirmy spines,
under their armpits, his face tilted,
assessing the giggles, careful
not to go too far.
If they wanted to make it stop,
they had to say, *Snowball,*
and instantly he'd back away.
Snowball, they'd shout, grins wide,
then *Snowflakes,* the code
for *Again*!

Bashful, all buttoned-up
in my best frock, inside me
a three-year-old yearns
to sidle close.

Snowflakes! She cries,
Come on, *Snowflakes!*

Story Belts

Transmutations
enchanted me; lovers
become mountains, brothers become swans.
But how to spring you
from the spell that held you captive?

Weeks, trussed up
in your recliner, protesting
you couldn't move, couldn't come
to the Adirondacks with me, next thing

you were
squeezing my thigh, belting out
"Wild Thing" with the radio, caved
in our blue sedan
as the valley sank below.

That day I was so intent
on visiting the Six Nations Museum—
without you, I'd have missed the bears.

You spotted them
as soon as you got out of the car.
A furry hump halfway
up a white pine, cub on her back.

You leapt around like a boy, waving your cap
to passing cars. You, great bear of a man,
flopped on your belly beside the highway,
binoculars raised.

What did the old man see in you,
that got us invited in?

A blue-jeaned elder, finger to his lips,
shrugged,
My wife don't like me bringing folk in here.

Stepping through to a screened back porch,
a raucous *Yaw, Yaw,*
birch trees laden, ravens all astir.

You clasped my elbow, to point—

a black bear on hind legs, taller than a man,
a few meters from my nose. Claws tore
at lard spiked to a slab of wood.
Nostrils flared, jet eyes glared, his pink
tongue curled around fat.

The shiver of a glance between us.

Still straddled safely
in the pine, the mother bear
waited her turn, clutch of small paws at her neck.

I feed them. You're not supposed to.
The old man gestured towards the thickening sky.
The winter will be long and hungry.
Winters, when this man beaded the story belts
strung, wall-to-wall in the museum.

Giant wings flexed and soared.
Into the pulse of wind, a shower
of ochre leaves.

Your face, transfixed, all sparkle
and shadow, like the flash of tawny fur
slinking through the bush.

When I wonder why
I stay, this is why I stay.

The bear
dropped onto all fours. Swaggered off
like a storm, twigs and branches
splintered in his wake.

III

Do I contradict myself?
Very well then I contradict myself,
(I am large, I contain multitudes.)

– Walt Whitman

Life after Life

after W. S. Merwin

If I hadn't drowned,
a ginger-haired sailor of seventeen,
after our ship was torpedoed,
if I hadn't gotten drunk on my birthday
and signed up with my mates,
hadn't run away from my war-worn mother
in Manchester and my pregnant sister,
hadn't been cursed with freckles and a baby face,
if I hadn't been sodomized by six able
seamen in a closet off the engine room,
hadn't prayed for Hitler
to kill us all and leapt
into the diesel-spilt flaming waves,
if I hadn't sunk below the screams
to stillness and vowed;
I'll never be a man again,

I would not have been born
ten years later
into a Manchester hospital;
a baby girl.

And if that little girl hadn't married
a man who could see past lives
and if he hadn't wrapped his arms around her,
voice to her ear, and guided her through
to the moment when the curtain fell
and rose again, where all the sailors, the bombers,
the pilots, stood together, the stage crowded,
and Seymour, our British sailor-lad at the centre,
all holding hands and taking a deep bow
to ear-shattering applause and getting drunk
together at the cast party, if he hadn't listened
to her tell and tell again

until her breath was free of shame,
until it was just another drama,
then she might have believed death
is the end of it.

Tasting Time

Tasting time in a kiss…
– Kenneth Slessor

Like charcoal and roses,
lemons and sulphur,
your lips with the flavour

of fish, of olives,
of snow, your lips
burn through
lifetimes, taste of sweat,
taste of oil.

In a skiff, the sea roiling,
on shore, lilacs and blood,
you with a spear in one hand,
you with a rifle, your lips in the dark

under canvas, on a mountain cliff,
taste of granite, your skin shrivelled,
lips cold, eyes lustreless.

Kiss of toes, of ankles, of nose,
dreaming your kiss.
Kiss of bone.

Kisses sprinkled—
ash on my tongue.

Other Lives

Great is the power of memory, exceedingly great, oh my God, a spreading limitless room within me. Who can reach its uttermost depths?

– Augustine, *Confessions*

I've watched a man give birth.
So visceral, I squatted
behind him, ready to catch the child.
When it was over, he wept.
All men should experience this,
he kept repeating.

I've seen a pale neck redden
in welts as a woman recalled
a sixteenth century hanging as a witch,
and her own birth, almost strangled
by the cord.

Traceries of other lives arise
unbidden, so I wasn't surprised
when my husband described his stabbing neck
ache like a sharpened stick thrust
through his throat.

We were at Black's Beach, Encinitas, had just
gotten out of the car. He hunched, head hung
slightly to the left, face
in a grimace.

A yam stick. We both pictured it.
The heft, the burnt design rough in my palms.
He smelt wood smoke, heard the hiss of flames.

Together, like a shared dream un-scrolling…

A glimpse of rainforest.
He was the man I loved, then as now.

His arms clinging
after the accident left him lame.

The tribe had travelled on. Our hungry children,
his ardent gaze. I was the wife who must act,
the one who betrays.

I waited for him
to recognize, to name
me culprit, his face eclipsed with pain.

He refused
my offer of a massage, lover's hands now,
assassin's then. He strode
the length of the beach alone.
The strange sense of revision.

I didn't yet know what it meant.
Who we were.
Who we would become.

Don't Say it

Not in your mother tongue,
diction
quick and soft and hushed,
not Kalahari style with plosive clicks,
or in a guttural throat purr.

Even the sibilant whisper,
the soft palate hum
would startle that wagtail's plucky strut
and the pair of wonga pigeons
rustling in the brush.
It would interrupt the canticle of crows,
the dithering of pines.

Your words would make
the searing sky grow pale,
the distant hills darken.

Sit here with me and breathe
the inarticulate blessings
as damp rises and the sun sets.

The heat of your palm on my knee
—is enough.

Going South

You could always sense
when a movie was about to
go south, as you called it.

We'd set out with eager expectations:
a romantic dinner, then settle into plush chairs
a box of popcorn to share.

Sometimes it was just after the credits,
other times deeper in, popcorn finished,
squeezing hands, leaning forward,
when you'd excuse yourself,
to the toilet or for another bottle of water
and I knew you wouldn't be back.

Remember Robert Redford in *The Horse Whisperer*,
how I stumbled into the foyer, into your waiting
arms, doubled over with sobs?
Don't ever leave me alone in a movie like that.
But that's a promise you refused to make.

Once the violins crescendo
and they bring in the cello,
you're gone.

Small Gusts of Suffering

This morning I want to say to you—remember,
that argument we used to have
about pain and suffering, how I'd say it's all
part of the human package, we can't know joy
until we've been broken open, but you
didn't see the point.

And I want to say—remember
that morning 30 years ago
when I insisted on an early start so
I drove while you dosed,
through small towns, stop and go lights,
past empty malls. I was fractious and ghosted
by the night's dreams, how strange I felt,
that violent urge to veer left,
to smash the car into a concrete abutment,
my foot pressed on the gas, eye on a brick wall,
the sound of crushed metal and breaking glass.
What a struggle it was to pull over
into a vacant lot, shut the motor off.

I wanted a hug, but you refused.
You saw darkness around me, a sticky cloud
you wouldn't touch.
"Go hug that tree," you told me, which is how
I ended up throwing my arms around
the knobbly bark of an oak, staring up
through bare branches at the leaden sky.
Cheek against the trunk, my skin felt melded
into bark, my flesh stiffening into cambium, an umbrella
of roots at my feet, a rumbling sound,
as gusts of suffering with Goya faces,
rippled through me; my ancestors, my descendants,
mouths contorted, eyes bulging.
I willed it all to sluice through me,
sink into the soil.

How long was it before the stillness,
a heart swell of appreciation?
The sky had brightened.
As I stepped away, you pointed up
and I spotted them, like blooms, each branch
studded with black feathered crows
watching me.

In Praise of Foibles

He wore his imperfections lightly,
announced them to strangers in the park.
He was his own blooper reel, a bank
of dispensations when the rest of us
screwed up.

He slept in his clothes for days and then
jumped into the pool to wash them.

When someone cut him off in traffic
he wouldn't snarl or curse, but think
of something he'd done worse
and forgive them both.

When he bid on a construction job,
his price was low with a proviso,
his gusto could (and probably would)
suddenly flag. No guarantees when the work
would be done, but his company was fun.

He could trash a hotel room
in seconds flat, socks strewn
over lampshades, sheets pulled loose,
pillows tossed. His own lair
was a fug of detritus and, when he first
moved in, lugging boxes of unpaid taxes
and bills, I prayed for strength.

He was the H in humble though he had
hubris, too, when the switch flipped
and his slick self rose from the ashes of defeat.
Revitalised, he became a whirl of industry.

And when I asked for a divorce,
he said he understood, he'd divorce
himself if he could.

Five years, we travelled separate
shores untangling what was his,
what was hers,
until we were clear,
our divorce had been a failure.
Although love meant more paperwork,
we volunteered for another round.

Wild Ponies

When my mother advised,
I tame
my capricious son,
like breaking a horse,

I felt the colt in me
kick. It whinnied and cantered off.
The harness I wore at two
tugged back my shoulders.
All the ways she'd corralled me
until I lay down, defeated.

My unruly hair,
"mane" she called it, pulling
my braids so tight, my ears raised.

She was terrified
of horses. Her feral father plopped
her onto his polo pony, then slapped
his rump.

Only you
recognized the wild pony
in me, long left languishing.

Your nickering heart
woke my own. My devotion
to our unfettered hours
ambling through thickets and meadows.

Of course, we were not ponies,
but parents.

You ignored the bills.
I paid mine early.
Pathologically responsible, you teased.

In truth, you were smitten
with my school teacher allure,
loved shaking loose the pins,
rinsing your face in my hair.

When my son ran off to follow
The Grateful Dead,
I could think of no cure
except to take more risks myself.

Rampant love in the dunes,
on a log in the woods in winter,
in the vermillion tube-slide
at the playground.

The nudist colonies we visited.
Volleyball in the buff.
The dance contest's unwritten
dress code; body jewellery,
chains around hips, baubles on nipples.
Not one tattoo, we, alone, gyrated
starkly unadorned. And won!

My long-dead mother phones,
Everything under control, dear?
From his bucking bronco, my son
waves his Stetson hat.

Now that you've trotted off,
who'll entice me
into mischief?

No Brakes!

I'm shouting, car
careening, foot
stomping the sheets.
I swerve

around jackhammer
men-at-work. You sprawl
on the hood, laughing,
like Micky Mouse on the run,

the old chartreuse Gremlin,
slaloming
signs and shovels.

I'm white-knuckling the wheel
up over the curb,
ploughing through green.

You could say I'm still trying
to steer you
with your old joke,

My problem is…
my wife does understand me.

Your dreams were darting
swallows in flight.
I could end this one differently—
the car sprouting wings.

Our Covenant

Tangled as we sometimes were
in discord, padlocked,
shackled and chained,

if one of us was sane
enough to call it,
we'd both drop everything.

Stop
and breathe together.

Dive into the warm sea
of the heart, sink below
the noose of thought.

With a Houdini's grace,
a dimensional shift.

Unloosed, we'd float
in the whispered wisdom
of the unseen.

As with a phantom limb, my body
still throbs for yours.
My mind stumbles

over your old boots, no longer
in the hall. Seated now,
beside your empty chair,

I hear your call.
I'll meet you there.

Anand, from beyond

It wasn't a voice,
but an inner pull, stronger
than both my trembling hands.
Worn thin by the sandpaper of suffering,
it was time.

The body unpeeled, like stripping off
an ape costume to a clash of cymbals.

I sent you love and didn't agonize.
That was *your* business.

Hands reached for me, raised me out of myself.

Not angels exactly, a streak
of light, a whisper of wings, no feathers.

Cradled in a hammock,
I rested
from the pain in my chest, the shock
of my stopped heart. I had
to forgive myself.

My emotions flung off like flecks of ice.

Everything shimmers. The light
pearlescent as paint.
At first, familiar landscapes,
forests and lakes,
altering the scene at will.

I expand to encompass all
or shrink to a shred of dust.
Yes, I miss the discrete body.

I witness my life, other lives,
surprised at how brightly I burned.
Even while I slept,
my energy travelled and touched people.
My contribution was sometimes my lethargy,
a grounding rod, calming
the urge to fly. I was a brake
for the collective field.
Not a mistake, or an illness.

You scratch and I feel
your nails on skin, a thread of me
still incarnate.

You sitting there, listening to me, wrapped
in your black embroidered shawl.
It's the clothes you choose, even the length
of your breath coming in
drifting out...

A splinter of consciousness
like music
played blindfolded
by seven billion angels.

IV

Are you willing to be sponged out, erased, canceled, made no thing, dipped in oblivion? If not, you will never really change.

– D. H. Lawrence, *The Phoenix*

Winter Doldrums

One night, the poles shifted.
After months of perfect coupling,
the orbit wobbled.

His eyes, those hazel craters
of invitation, froze over.
Balm of his voice, tightened.
The rat-a-tat shotgun retort.
If only, she could seduce him
out of this madness, ease
his frayed nerves.

Slowly, she stripped off
her bra, shimmied her breasts,
but he didn't watch.
She slipped into bed, but he failed
to wrap his thighs around
her chilled feet.
She nuzzled with her cheek,
her favourite perch
on his heart, but he grunted
and flipped over.

She dared not breach
the wings of his back.
Swallowed her words.
Turned out the light.

Skating black ice, her thoughts
skidded out from under her.
She heard the surface crack.

Panic Attack

He doesn't want to go
into the hospital.
His quaking palm in mine
sweaty, the air cold.
An autumn night,
laps around the parking lot,
old brick hospital, a sprawl
of new wings, checkerboard of lit-up squares.
He shudders at the howl
of an ambulance as we pass the ER.
It's only your mind. It's not real. He knows,
but it doesn't help.

We climb the small slope to where oaks
tremble and a blood moon blinks.
Scent of fine rain
on pavement. Lamp posts hum
with ghosts. His eyes flit, startled sparrows,
abandons my hand and bolts
towards the glass doors.
He's told me how they tourniquet
his thoughts with drugs, TV, and the *sugar coma;*
all the cookies he can eat.
Pulls his jacket tighter, hesitates,
then pivots, veering
back to me.

By dawn, the sky clears. He slumps
into my arms, agrees
to go back home.
Flopping into bed, he sleeps, while I
unknot my own breath, my palm
pinned to the wild rabbit
trapped inside my chest.

Before Blast-Off

I feared it was a mistake,
but I couldn't resist.
I'd watched him for hours out in the barn
sorting his tools, his back
slumped, head down, with me hidden
behind the kitchen curtains so as not
to soften my resolve, when every sinew
of my being ached
to go out there, and then, finally, I did.
A haze of rain glazed his face and mine,
but we stayed there anyway. His liquid pupils pulled
me into deep space, the swirl of galaxies,
that fourth dimensional shift
we'd colonized, afloat side by side, buoying
each other up
as our various children
and grandchildren tugged at us like satellites.
In my dreams, I was strapped into a rocket ship,
the countdown already begun. I could see him
waving from the control room.
For years, gazing
into each other had been our home port,
and now, I was selling up, migrating
to Australia without him.
I wanted to rewind the film, swallow back
the impulse for free fall.
We stood, suspended
in the undeniable affection between us.
Even if we never laid
eyes on each other again in this life,
this look would sustain me, reassure me
I wasn't abandoning
him or myself, just following
the next natural step into the rainforest
to face alone on my first day, a pack of feral dogs

that killed the goats
on the property where I settled,
a python under foot as I climbed the ladder
to bed, and six months later, a dislocated shoulder
as I hefted a bunch of bananas down the mountain trail.
I nursed the image of his gaze through all of that,
my body alien without his touch and yet grateful
to have been loved, craving only
the circle of his arms for comfort.
At 2 am, when my shoulder pain consumed me,
the phone rang. His voice surfaced
all the way from San Diego. "I tried to hold you off,"
he said, "But, finally, I surrendered."

Belonging

She follows
the flickering beam, thrill
goosing her arms,
alone in the dark.

She trains her light
on a patch of ground, stomps
to scare off
imagined snakes, flops
flat on her back, arms
akimbo in the top paddock,
crushed grass beneath her, a churn
of stars above.

Clouds slip-stream across
the moon. Squabbling flying foxes,
circus of cicadas.

She has unmarried herself
from the brambles of family,
stripped off her bark, whiff of melancholy
and lemon-scented gum.
The warm red dirt candles her spine.

She breathes in this welcome,
migrant, far from her birthplace,
stranger under the Southern Cross.

Her body has altered
in this succulent landscape. It has bled
for the last time here.
Streak by streak, illuminated
dust reminds her,
she has merely
borrowed it, this space capsule,

an uneasy captain, host—
for multitudes,

microbes spin through her bowels,
more of them than human cells, bacteria
invisible
in viscera and skin.

Above her, history in free fall,
burning itself out
before it re-congeals.

Star dust and fluid,
what she's made of,
has sprinkled these soils,
tumbled over
these cliffs in long
spindles of light and water,

until she appears

to be lying there, tracking
meteors, the glint of her eyes
flaring like a struck match.

Prelude to an Afternoon Nap

Your freckled Irish skin, with its multiple
flavours; bitter apricots,

your lopsided grin
ever amazed at the bounty of my breasts,

the frisson of awe:

our limbs roll into and over each other
as if caught in a mountain stream
gathering force, your beard

a tickle I barely notice,
a tangle of hands and breath.

In the lush forest of your gaze
like when we met, I catch

a rare glimpse of something wild
that startles and flies off.

Your eyes, I've studied these thirty years
and will never comprehend.

The thrill of your strangeness, I'm immersed
in the thrust of our differences.
My pelvic squeeze,

voltage amplified with age.

Who could have imagined
ripening together like this?

Poof

after Dorianne Laux

Motoring northwest to Carnarvon Gorge away from the surf,
through arid plains, skinny beef cattle and the occasional calf,
a detour before Christmas with the grandkids, van stuffed,
John Denver's "Coming of the Roads", anthem of grief,
voices braiding, my warbling soprano, your bass gruff,
my hand at rest on your thigh. Warm air carries a whiff
of diesel and manure, me feeling content with myself
unprepared for the flare up, your sudden huff,
cinder from a previous grumble sparks a rift
the chisel of your point of view and my wheedling tiff,
my jaw tight, your eyes squinting for roos, your tone aloof,
the trap of your logic, my rebuttal not clever enough,
when you shout, Whoosh—and poof
our skull bones shift, we're lifted up through the van roof
replaced by two fourth dimensional beings who doff
a dossier of our history. They hover observing; my back stiff,
your white-knuckled grip on the wheel—and with a guttural laugh
slip back into our bodies, pull onto the verge and turn the motor off.
Smoothing the contours of my damp cheeks, you wonder if
we can start afresh. Your fervent fingers, cool and rough.

A Bargain

A deal at half the price.
You email a photo
as proof: this once in a lifetime,
only you can spot it, treasure
beneath the asbestos cladding,
sagging porch, aluminium windows,
stumped on concrete blocks,
slightly out of plumb—beach shack.

You stand in the foreground,
unveiling your magic trick,
ta-da, arms extended, fingers thrust out
like antennae, your entire face luminous
with a toothy grin.

The pitch of your voice
rises, your tempo speeds,
a froth of possibilities I clearly don't get.
You are Jack, come home
without the cow,
these magic beans
our fortune now.

Blue Mania

Their breath is agitation, and their life
a storm whereon they ride, to sink at last…
– Lord Byron

I'm listening, but not
to his words exactly, more to the rise of pitch,
the static crackle,
his voice on the phone, flint on flint.
From his van in Florida, the man I love, announces
his plans. I stand alone
on a wharf in Australia.
Swooping overhead, white cockatoos shriek.

Just come home. My mind is scrambling
for words to salvage this. *Are you sleeping?*
It's the wrong question, a barrage of reasons
why sleep is no longer required.
Awake at 4 am, he ran ten miles before
meditating to receive this latest guidance.
Today, it was to buy food and distribute it
amongst the homeless. Now he'd like to set up a shelter.
And, no, he will not come home.
He is possessed again
by the turbulent stranger.

I try to focus
on the grey legs and webbed feet of a pelican
who paces with his eye on a fisherman's bucket.
I picture my husband's plump, freckled legs,
his flat feet I've cradled in my lap and kissed.

You always try to control me.
You're toxic, you're not spiritually evolved enough
to understand.

It's true.
I'll never understand.
Thirty years of his tidal rips
and I'm still caught and spun under.

The sea is dead calm,
beneath my feet, the jetty shudders.

Waking Slow

Gradually he relinquished
the texture of bark, scent
of pine needles in snow,
the loam of freshly turned soil.
The fiddler's waltz felt funereal
to him then. The variegated grain
of a slab of rosewood failed
to rouse him to turn on his lathe.
He travelled to Yosemite
and never got out of the car.
And when he returned, the children, clambering
in and out of his lap, were all too much for him.
Eyes glazed, dreams banished, he retired
to the blue light of a screen to blot out his imaginings,
old sit-coms he used to watch as a boy,
the familiar surf
of laugh tracks rising and falling.
Ticking off the hours, he woke
only to wait,
until his bones were weary enough
to sink (as he'd say)
into something cosy, like a coma.
That void-defying void.

Untethered

I admit
there was a trickle of relief
when I understood

the worst that could happen

had finally happened, exactly
as he'd described, more than twenty
years before:

the rope, the van, parked
on a deserted road, the message
for the police, so no one

who loved him, would find him

it was his "get out of jail free" card,
this choice, he made each morning
not to, and it was my job

or I volunteered—to lure him
his siren of the kitchen, Scheherazade,
a talent honed

from performing "happy
childhood" to assuage
my parents' grief.

By that February, I'd grown
inured to dread, had sprinted
to the beach at dawn

and returned
to a trail
of urgent messages.

He'd promised to make
contact, if he could. In my dreams,

my tongue explores the pulse
in his neck, heat
of his breath.

Truth is, I'm clinging still—
knots that do not hold.

Legacy

Permission to quack,
even when there are no ducks,

to plop on the floor of Boston Market
with three-year-olds, singing, *All fall down*,

even if you're balding and built
like Papa Bear.

Permission to never
be appropriately dressed for any social situation.

To breed dust balls and spiders
and never spring clean.

To belt out "Monday Morning Blues"
even on Thursday.

To disregard the injunction and yes—
Be Ridiculous.

To proclaim every season—
good sleeping weather.

To impersonate Santa Claus with your own beard,
but tell everyone you're actually his brother.

To play Christmas carols all day, all year round.

To quietly fail and cut your losses,
but broadcast the wins.

Permission to laugh at your *foibles*,
(your favourite word) and teach the kids how
to turn whining into competitive sport.

To recognise when it's time to leave—
music's too caustic, the film violent
or it's all too much—

to say, *I love you, but I need to leave now*,
and do it.

Again

Yesterday, before dawn
I was crucified again.

The iron spikes were thoughts
biting soft flesh.

A toothache of fear, the panic-bell clang,
the Judas kiss of self-betrayal.

When the death bird swooped in
to peck loose
the string bag of my beliefs

everything tight and knotted
fell away.

In the space between
I discovered

my untouched self.

Splinter

You can't fix it—
the tsunami in your heart after his death,
the flux and stillness in its wake.

Sun torching the pasture.
The stubborn ground parched to dust.

You can't fix—
The ice storm in Portland, calved
off glaciers in the Arctic.

Your sister's cancer. At the healer, her wish—
a peaceful death.

Then brightness
splinters your dark corners.

You know you're here to be
broken. Nothing to fix.

Not the rift between you
and the sun, not the one
between you and the sea.

Afterglow

The late afternoon light
is phosphorescent,
air like fiery raindrops
and in that field, the absence
of the old white horse
is palpable.

Under the fig tree
where the ground is trampled,
grasses rise to meet his sway-backed
erasure. Branches droop.
Leaves ripple in the wind
as dust-flecks spin.

Molecules adjust to the shape
of emptiness.
No urgency—to fill in
what was there.

The invisible
made visible
in trembling points of light
and the distant echo of hooves.

Manufactured by Amazon.com.au
Sydney, New South Wales, Australia
Printed on the traditional lands of the Dharawal Peoples

32975710R10046